"2021"

To: Val
From: Windy
happy birthday

BLESSINGS
IN UNCERTAIN TIMES

GOD IS ALWAYS PRESENT

CLARENCE KD McNAIR

ISBN-13: 978-1-7361198-7-7

For information regarding special discounts for bulk purchases, please contact LaBoo Publishing Enterprise at staff@laboopublishing.com

Table of Contents

Dedication

This book is dedicated to you. I hope it strengthens your faith especially in these uncertain times. This is a great step toward your faith walk, especially when it appears that there is no light shining around you or in your life.

I just want to remind you that God is always present, so don't give up when the pressure seems to overwhelm you and life looks hopeless. Just remember, sometimes we overlook the blessings right in front of our face because maybe they did not come in the form that we expected. So take a second, open your eyes, and in just a matter of time you will see God's favor if you just have a little faith and keep believing. Now get some tea or coffee, and go to a quiet place and enjoy *my God experience*!

Acknowledgments

I want to thank God for giving me the vision to see his work in my life and other people's lives during very dark and uncertain times in the world. To my family and supporters, thank you, this has been a long journey of many sleepless nights putting this book together. Sometimes, God would wake me up out of my sleep at night to write. It was a very supernatural experience throughout this whole production.

A special thank you to Latisha Wilborne. Your story is an example of blessings in uncertain times. Your daughter Bella is a reminder to the world that God is still present. May God continue to bless her heart.

To my sister Candice, keep up the good work, you have handled this pandemic very well by leaning on your faith and walking with God.

To my brother Antoine, it's not easy taking care of a family, especially during times of uncertainty. However, you still get up every day to go to work in the medical field and contribute to helping others in need outside of your family. God bless you for putting your life on the line to help others. We appreciate you, and just know that God will reward you for your service.

To all the new mothers, this has been a crazy time for you with everything going on in the world. However, never forget that the Lord is your strength and he understands what 2020 has been like for you. Just remember his Word. He will never leave you nor forsake you, meaning you're never alone. He hears and he knows what you need and he will supply the strength you need.

To all my entrepreneurs in the world, all my creative people who figured it out, God bless you all. Many of you have been able to thrive in uncertainty and I commend your faith.

Special thank you to all the men and fathers who reached out to help those in need.

Special thank you to all the essential workers around the world.

To my praying warriors, thank you.

To my wife, your prayers gave me the extra fuel that I needed to complete this project, thank you.

To my publishing family, thank you Kimmoly and the team for everything.

To my sister Francine and niece Cassara, keep the faith— God is with you all the time.

To Malacka, keep touching the people.

To Grandma Pauline, Grandma Marry, and Grandma Ms. Lou, we miss you all, thanks for all the years of prayers you gave. To my kids, Amaria, Khori, and Marley, make sure this book is passed down to your kids, kids, kids. Daddy loves you all.

Thank you Amber, you have a heart of gold.

Thank you Pinky Cole for leading by example, showing people and entrepreneurs that anything is possible no matter what's going on in the world.

To my cousin Tugga, we are praying for you, we didn't forget about you, God is with you, I'm praying for you.

To one of my biggest supporters and family, Nathaniel, aka Dugga, we're almost there.

Dr. Sean McMillan, the interview we did at the beginning of the pandemic opened a major door, thank you.

To my barber, Derrick Green, aka, Dee, I'm blessed to get haircuts and have spiritually uplifting conversations at the same time. Thank you for being who you are.

Thank you Mila Thomas for always showing support.

A special thank you to my spiritual warrior sister, Cora Jakes Coleman, you are a blessing. Thank you for believing in me. Words can't express the level of gratefulness that I have for you. Thank you so much for being a part of this project.

Last but not least, I'd like to give a special thanks and prayer to all of the people who may not agree with me, who may not understand me, who may have something against me, or maybe just do not like me. In this world, not everyone will like you. However, I pray for you all. I wish you blessings, peace, and prosperity, and I hope after reading this book you will have a new perspective on my experiences and the messages and how I see life. God is love and he wants us to love all, even those who disagree.

Foreword

Let me first tell you, the mere fact that you have opened this book, and are reading it, comes because of an uncertain blessing. As an author, pastor, and daughter of the mega-church pastor T.D. Jakes, and my amazing mother, First Lady Serita Jakes, my schedule is uncertain. I received this request from Clarence in this uncertain time and didn't think I would have the time to write, but I started reading this book and couldn't put it down. *Blessings in Uncertain Times* is a book that does not just challenge you to be in the moment, but more importantly, be in the moment, and make sure that it impacts your life and the lessons you gain from it. It is effortless to allow this pandemic to put pressure on you, and quite frankly, cause you to collapse completely. Your author Clarence will enable you to have your real emotions and real experiences, but he does not condone your pity party.

He doesn't leave you wondering what you should do, but he gives you scriptures you can stand on. He gives you practical tools to examine your life and situation. He allows you into the depths of his experiences while still being able to share the flexibility and transparency of his wisdom, and somehow, you walk away with the strength to carry on even without really ever expecting that response to come from this book. This book draws you closer to your relationship realities by forcing you to stop making excuses and beginning to zoom into how this uncertain time can benefit you. The thing I love about this book is that it is timeless.

Though I am sure that during this pandemic season, it is fair to say this is an uncertain time for both myself and Clarence, I am confident in knowing that uncertain times are coming again. This book helps to remind you of what you should rely on in uncertainty. This book makes you slow down and take the time to build and develop you, in God, and not just in these uncertain times, but in the uncertain times to come that happen in life. You will receive a strategy for uncertain times that you will be able to carry on even long after the 2020 pandemic is over. Something that resonated with me in this book is the power of what I call a spiritual resume. The way that Clarence puts it is, "Do not forget God's past faithfulness when faced with worry." It's essential that when times come to bring us down, we look to the times that have happened before that made us feel like we would never make it, and you reading this already calls that time a liar.

You have to understand that sometimes God doesn't rescue us from a thing, but He protects us from the situation by not letting it kill us. Sometimes, in uncertain times, all you can look to be grateful for is this moment right now, this moment that God has given you to breathe, to take this day in and allow it to teach you something that makes life worth just breathing. As long as you are breathing, you call every agenda and weapon of the enemy a lie. This book offers you the escape you need to breathe, relax, and permit yourself to experience God in a way that you haven't been willing to experience before. This book allows you to examine your surrender's power and what it will look like to embrace the reality that you have to stop looking for you in God and start looking for God in you. Your author Clarence is going to unlock the power of your belief.

This book is prepared to empower you and motivate you to pick your dreams back up, even in devastation, and attack your destiny. Sometimes, the things that come to shake us have come to bring us closer to God and groom us for the wisdom built in the grits and grief of life. Whether you lost your job or just lost your way in this uncertain time, there is a blessing for you, and your author can testify to it. Sometimes, when you need God to seal a thing for you in an uncertain time, He shows up. Now, if that doesn't prepare you, did I mention my absolute favorite part of the book by far?

There are 20 enemies of faith listed in one of the first few chapters of the book. As the author of *Faithing It and Ferocious Warrior*, with a chapter on "Ferocious Faith", I can testify that these enemies are valid, and if you examine them, learn them, and overcome them, you will walk your way into *Blessings in Uncertain Times*. Enjoy this read. I know I did.

Cora Jakes-Coleman

Introduction

This season is forcing us to switch roles with people who live with restrictions every day and have lives that are totally dependent upon God and his strength. During this crisis of financial struggles and medical issues, I encourage you to use this time to reflect, rebuild, and come face-to-face with yourself. This book is a tool to help you overcome the fear of this moment and develop gratitude in the midst of an epidemic. Be grateful for the time to slow down and reap the benefits of the things we take for granted, and see God show up in a time when we need him the most. You will see that God works best when you let him take the driver's seat. You may now turn the page and experience this moment from a faith-driven viewpoint. I'm sure it will be life-changing for you.

CHAPTER 1
God Has Been Here All Along

One thing is for certain: this pandemic has taught us we've never needed a building to receive God's blessings. He's always been available to us, no matter where you are. God is always present in any circumstance, we just have to slow down, be still and listen. In the past, everyone was so accustomed to moving 100 miles an hour that it was hard for any of us to hear God with all of the noise and distractions around. However, every now and then he will put us in a situation where we have no choice but to slow down and experience him. I think it's safe to say 2020 was that year for most of us in the world.

The saying "Be careful what you pray for because you just might get it" might be an understatement at this point. I believe so many prayers were answered this year. The part where it gets a little tricky is when we recognize that God answered the prayers you were praying for, they just didn't present themselves in the form you thought they would. Remember sitting in rush-hour traffic at 5 AM every morning, Monday through Friday, praying God would make a way to where you could work from home or stay home with your children and still work? Remember when you prayed and asked God if you could spend more time in the kitchen to cook your own food because eating out was killing your wallet? Remember when it was hard to help others because your restaurant bill looked like a mortgage every month, so you couldn't save a dime from eating out and buying gas after paying your bills? Little did we know, we were about to experience God in a whole different way, and get a perspective of those who live on limitations and restrictions every day. We would then learn how for some, God is their everything. Ask yourself, "How can I truly experience the power of God if he is not my main source of power?" What I've come to realize is that God does not operate under the same clock or time that we operate, but God's timing is always right on time. Even if it doesn't make sense to you, I'm sure you're wondering: why did God pick the pandemic to show up and show out? For years, you have been trying to have more time to get closer to God, but for some reason you just never made time to slow down and feel God's presence. That was me for many years as well; running on and off trains and planes, always busy, until I ended up hitting a brick wall emotionally and mentally from almost burning myself out. I had no choice but to turn to God once I drained all of my energy.

Like most of us, it took a lot for us to slow down and be quiet to hear God's voice. The pandemic made everything stop! All of a sudden, we had to live without live concerts, ball games, summer conventions, yearly family vacations and movie nights, family hugs, grandma's kisses, sending the kids off to school, social events. Everything all stopped and got put on hold! It was time for us to allow God to take the center stage. Many of us felt like we were Daniel in the lion's den, wondering if God had forgotten about us. However, just before everything totally fell apart, he showed up right at your breaking point. I'm expressing this because often-times we pray so much for God's direction and blessings in tough times as if he's not already aware of our struggles, pain, concerns and fears. We forget he is the great creator who has all power in his hands. Just as there are horrible stories and bad news, there are just as many amazing stories of people who experienced God in a whole new way while experiencing the most uncertain challenges of their lives. I would often read and hear people say, "No need to worry, God's got us." For most of us, it's easier said than done, especially when you're no longer in control of the outcome. Life starts to look like one big scary movie with you starring as the main character. The truth is, we were never in control of anything, and that's the most interesting part about life. We think we know what tomorrow may bring, and we think we know what the future may hold for us, but we fail to keep an open mind of the unknown.

Oftentimes, we feel the vision of things working out in the best way. I'm sure there's been times in your life when something worked out totally different than what it was you were expecting. Sometimes, it becomes frustrating, disappointing and hurtful, but the reality is that once you can get past that moment in your life, you'll look back and realize God was trying to get your attention and talk to you the whole time. No one wants to deal nor walk in the direction of the storm; instead, we usually try to run from it. Yet, some storms in life are impossible to escape. I call them the "speed bumps." No matter how fast you're going, they'll stop you. God wants you to know that what you've been seeking is why you are where you are emotionally. He gives us the solution to help us overcome even after we give up on ourselves. That answer is to let go and let God take the driver's side. We have to open the door for God to totally be in charge. Most of us have enough history with God that we should not let worry drive us crazy and let emotions control us. Don't allow worrying to interfere and cause you to fear what you cannot control. It may be best to write a letter on all the good that has happened to us, so that we are reminded of the blessings we have when we began to worry. Remember all of the times in the past of uncertainty when God showed up.

Do not forget God's past faithfulness when faced with worry. The worry of today or a crazy moment makes us second guess if God will be there tomorrow. All we need to do is do all we can do about today and trust God for tomorrow. When negative thoughts come into the speck of your mind and try to get you to worry, say no to those thoughts. Tell yourself, "I did all I can do today, and I'm trusting in God for tomorrow. I'm not going to let stress and worry drive me to places I have no business going. I will walk into tomorrow confident that my God is walking with me, and whatever his will is will be done anyway. I must seek his kingdom above all things, and the rest is in his hands." The point I am making is that, when the world doesn't make sense or when life appears to have failed you, let go and allow yourself to experience God in a way that you've never experienced him before. Remember: every trial will cause us to experience God in many different ways.

CHAPTER 2
Trust God Even When Life Doesn't Make Sense

What you know will sooner or later override your feelings. Wisdom blocks wrongful thinking. Sometimes, we can become addicted to ill feelings and not realize how, in those hard times, we have one million things racing through our minds. We may feel so unsafe that we don't realize how certain of our feelings may have nothing to do with the promises God has for today and tomorrow. It is we whom emotions and feelings change from day-to-day. We unfortunately go into everything with that same approach and perspective. At some point, we have to come to the realization that God does not operate like we do. It does not matter how you feel about the truth, the truth is the truth. You are not what you feel, you are what you believe. Your feelings will catch up to what you believe if you're firm and dedicated to what you believe.

Where the mind goes, the man follows. It's no wonder why in the darkest times, we actually don't expect anything to work out. We don't expect to be able to get past these moments because we feel powerless, afraid, confused, and uncertain. These feelings and emotions cause us to give up the hope in God's ability to show up in our craziest time of need. It would be weird if God changed his mind daily on being here for us, as if he's going to be in a bad mood or something when we call on him. Fortunately, he's not like us human beings. We are oftentimes limited from possibilities and growth because of the feelings that become roadblocks in our lives, rather than operating on the facts and staying firm in our belief. Remember, you are not alone in this moment. It may be hard and even challenging, but you just have to continue to believe that God is still walking with you, holding your hand even when you don't feel it.

2 Corinthians 10:5 KJV states "casting down imaginations, and every high thing that   exalteth itself against the knowledge of God, and bringing into captivity every thought to the obedience of Christ." This verse helped me many times in my life when my thoughts started to attack my beliefs. I had to remind myself of this Bible verse in times of uncertainty. It took my faith and vision to understand things clearly. One day, a friend of mine got a call from their job telling them they were no longer needed.

My friend became really stressed and upset. Although they were hurt from losing the job, this particular friend was then reminded of all the times they talked about starting their own business. They had all of these great ideas for a new business, but put it off for many years because they felt they didn't have time to work and start a business at the same time. Putting their dreams to the side caused them to lose the motivation to work on anything. But on that particular day, everything changed. My friend had to really think about what had just taken place. All of a sudden, he started to have an awakening that he was being pushed out of the job, so he could be pushed into what it is that he always wanted to do. Sometimes, it takes a crisis to save us from continuously wasting years and not fulfilling our God-given talents. Sometimes, you need a godly experience to take place, so that you have to totally rely on him to provide for you when the job security is out the door, or that person that you depended on is no longer available. Then, all alone, you become the answers you were looking for and God shows up the most for you.

I find one of the hardest things to do is to accept the fact that blessings may come from a person or particular situation in the craziest times. The blessings may not align with your beliefs. They could come in the form of a person who's dealing with their own challenges, or may not be seen as a God-fearing person, but in challenging times

God has a strange way of using unexpected persons to help you. Speaking from personal experience, I've received help from all kinds of people in the darkest hours of my craziest moments. Opportunities have come when I was a little scared, like there was no way God could be sending these people to help me. However, God was connecting me with them and gave me an opportunity to share his word. I communicated with people that I realized were those who might've needed some encouragement, while they brought resources that I needed. I may have met them so they could help me move forward to get past the storm. You just never know who is going to step in and grab you out of your craziest times. That person may not be sent to stay in your life, but they may just be sent for that particular moment to help you get what you need. It may not necessarily be what you want, but what you need at that time. **Hebrews 11:6 KJV** states, "But without faith it is impossible to please him: for he that cometh to God must believe that he is, and that he is a rewarder of them that diligently seek him."

With that being said, here are the **20 Enemies of Faith:**

1. Fear

2. Worry

3. Doubt: a feeling of uncertainty that God will keep his word. Doubt can be a powerfully destructive

force if we yield to it; it can eat away at our faith.

4. Lack of trust

5. Lack of studying God's word

6. Not devoting time for prayer

7. Holding on to problems you have no control over

8. Impatience

9. Human reasoning: the action of thinking about something in a logical, sensible way

10. Unforgiveness: when you choose not to forgive, you choose to keep yourself hostage of the past. You choose to block yourself from moving forward, and you choose to keep yourself from living the life that pleases God.

11. Failure to act upon God's word, especially when you know his word is true

12. Not standing firm to who you are; changing your ways to placate others

13. Constantly complaining

14. Not walking in love. The Bible says that God is love and everyone who does not love, does not know God.

15. Not taking action, which interferes with your faith being strengthened

16. Letting other people control your mood

17. Overworking yourself

18. Not being honest with yourself about your fears

19. Waiting around not doing anything to change your situation because in your mind things will get better on their own

20. Not watching what comes out of your mouth.

Proverbs 3:5-6 NIV states that you are to "Trust in the LORD with all your heart and lean not on your own understanding; in all your ways submit to him, and he will make your paths straight."

CHAPTER 3
Small Blessings

I know for many of us having to downsize is not easy. Some may have had to downsize their car, house, career, wardrobe or community. However, it allows us to look at life from a different angle to see the power of the small blessings. You may have been used to having it all, but sometimes in your season of growth you have to downsize to get to the other side. You never know, your perspective of the smaller blessings in your life may determine your growth. How many times have you been in situations where you had to let some things go? When we have a moment of uncertainty and challenges in our life, it's so easy to forget that there are people who live on restrictions every single day even when they are not in a rough time. These challenges are their normal life, and they don't even consider the possibility of the things that you have taken for granted. It may feel like it's the end of the world in your life, or you may feel lost, but even when you feel disappointed or tired, don't give up. You're one step away from growth, because there is a lesson in the storm. Yes, you may not have an umbrella big enough to handle this one, but remember that God controls the storm and he has the power to determine the amount of rain in our lives before he steps in. You have to tell yourself, "I'm not going to worry about tomorrow. Instead, I'm going to trust in the only one who can do anything about tomorrow." We know our Heavenly Father knows what we need. Looking back on the biggest lessons I've learned, I realize I've said this line about 1000 times when learning about the small blessings. Hence, small blessings don't necessarily mean "small" and can present themselves in many ways. We may not see things the way they really are, we may only see things based on where we are spiritually. This means the closer you get to God, the better your vision and perception of life becomes. You will begin to be less stressed as you see things the way God sees things. You will be able to appreciate the things that most people can't even see. Now on the flip side, the further away from God you are, the harder it is for you to see the small, hidden blessings in your life. Some may even experience a high level of stress, because spiritually you're not connected to the creator. Therefore, you cannot see things as God sees them; you will merely see life through the eyes of the world, which does not align with the thoughts of God. This was actually a personal experience for me many times in my life. I had to think back on when I was spiritually low and was not connected to the creator the way I should have been. I took on a lot of unnecessary stress that I did not even have to deal with, all because my thoughts were not mentally aligned with the word. For so long, I mentally suffered trying to understand in my own words what the Bible was saying years ago before my time. As **Luke 16:10 NIV** states, "Whoever can be trusted with very little can also be trusted with much…" As we can clearly see, your faith in those small experiences allows God to bless you for your obedience. Jesus said, "I know your tribulations and poverty (but you are rich)". The Christians, though poor, possessed riches far more valuable   than silver or gold. They were rich because of their faith and integrity in God.

CHAPTER 4
The Other Side
of the Storm

Have you ever thought about how the toughest storms in your life were just signs of you needing to reconnect with God? Just like a child who goes away from their parents, then returns back years later to reconnect with their maker. Most of us would go through a very difficult time to ignite our ability to experience a new life and reconnect with God. Sometimes, it's good to start all over and just take a whole different approach in how you move forward. Today, I can say that I'm glad I went through those tribulations, because there were people I needed to get out of my life, who are now all gone. **Joshua 1:9** urges us to be strong and courageous, and to not be frightened or dismayed for the Lord your God is with you wherever you go. **Deuteronomy 31:6** similarly urges us to be strong and have no fear or dread of them, because the Lord your God goes before you, he will be with you, he will not fail you or forsake you.

CHAPTER 5
Spiritually High Risk

Recently we've learned about what it means to be a high risk person as it relates to different viruses. However, there is another type of high risk that most people experience during their life and do not pay any attention to, and that is when their spirituality is low. Being at a low place spiritually puts you at risk of being attacked by the enemy at any given time. When you're spiritually weak, you become vulnerable; you become an easy target for Satan to attack you. The devil may try to get into your mind and inflict distractions, influence signs of spiritual malnutrition, confusion, encourage lingering thoughts that may haunt you from past mistakes, doubt, disrupt your sleep, anxiety, and more. The devil may try to get you to solve your own problems instead of trusting God, which could then lead to you falling backwards into something that you've already overcome.

Spiritual malnutrition occurs when you don't get enough spiritual food. When you hit a hard place, the devil tries to block you from seeing the light at the end of the tunnel. However, sometimes you have to be spiritually connected to the creator to ensure you can see the light. Your connection with God will help you to see things that only your spiritual eyes can envision. This may take some practice. Although they say time heals all, it really just covers up the emotions you've attached to the moment until the next falling out. Only a renewal of the mind heals, which means old habits must be changed to generate a new mindset. This is why God said we must renew the mind to think like him. Be transformed by the renewing of your mind (**Roman 12:2**). Think about it: if time healed all things, then a person would not still be having problems with past pain in their later age. It's not until the person gets help that they heal, then work on their thoughts and mind. Most people who hold things in and wait on time to heal all things, get worse and develop emotional disorders. It's not until they undergo spiritual transformation that they can then begin to heal. If you go through life with lots of emotional problems and keep covering up the hurt with external things, then you leave no choice but to fall into a dark place when things fall apart. Once you're in this dark place, you'll tend to lose all hope in what God is able to do. This dark place can make you feel like your problems are too big for God to fix.

Sometimes, we may even feel like God can't hear us, and our unresolved past traumas will somehow start to resurface. When this happens, they frequently send us into a downward spiral and we try to self-medicate. Don't become discouraged and hopelessly turn to things that will only bring a temporary fix. Most of the time, we go through our whole life depending on external things to bring us happiness and help us escape reality. This is when you become a prisoner to your emotions. This is a problem, because your emotions are a condition to respond to based on your past experiences. All of these things contribute to you being at high risk for spiritual attacks during uncertain times in your life. This is why it's very important for you to work on yourself constantly, because you never know what you may face day-to-day. In order for you to see God's blessings in the storm, you have to connect with him so you know there is a plan for you no matter what. All things will work out for the good of those who love the Lord, and he will not let you down. We just have to be honest and realize these much-needed situations put us in a position to rethink life and take a closer look at ourselves. No one on this earth is perfect, and we have all had situations to almost drive us over the hill. But these are required to help us make better decisions. God knows your heart and your story from the day you were born, so any wall you may hit in your life has already been worked out. Sometimes, in order to see it, we have to experience God's full power and go through tough moments to build our faith.

CHAPTER 6
Feeling Unworthy

Many people may feel unworthy and think God will not step in to help during the hard times. Many people look at the number of times that they did not feel that they had a connection with God. They may have felt their past sin and imperfections were punishment from God. All types of crazy thoughts go through our heads when things seem like they are not working out in our favor. Perhaps because of them you thought there was no way God would step in and rescue you. Coming from personal experience, these moments of uncertainty made me question if I was really worthy and hadn't done enough for God to receive his blessings. I started to wonder if I was to blame for what I was going through. I remember so many times being in a place of loss and just not feeling that I had been good enough for God, because of my mistakes and repeated mistakes. I felt like my prayers went unanswered. However, it was also in those moments that I remembered reading something that stated God can use anyone for his purpose, no matter what their situation is. Regardless of how bad you may have thought you were as a person, God is not the type to leave you when you're up against the wall. God is not punishing you, it's your lack of hope causing your destruction. God works in mysterious ways, and I've learned that during my life's storms, I came out better than what I was before I went in. During that storm, I could not see what God was doing, but I had to learn to trust him in the middle of ambiguity. He always has a bigger plan; you just have to believe, even if you feel unworthy. God is love and he loves you more than you could ever imagine. **Romans 5:8 ESV** states: "God shows his love for us in that while we were still sinners, Christ died for us." Never forget that verse. It shows us how much God loves us, so in those moments of doubt you can reflect on what the word says, and how even during our messed-up places of life and sinful ways he still loved us. **James 1:2-4 ESV** states: "Count it all joy, my brothers, when you meet trials of various kinds, for you know that the testing of your faith produces steadfastness. And let steadfastness have its full effect, that you may be perfect and complete, lacking in nothing." This part is important because it shows you that God always has a plan, and just because you may not be perfect or you may have had a rough past, don't let that hold you back in trusting God. You must have hope in the possibility that this rough place could be preparing you for an even better opportunity and preparing you for the next level of your life.

CHAPTER 7

Breakthrough

You only receive a breakthrough when you hit a wall. When we define these two words, we see that *break* means to separate or cause to separate into pieces as a result of a blow, shock, or stain (Oxford language). *Through* means to move into one side and out of the other side. In this place, we feel everything has dried up and have hit the end of our rope. However, it's in this very place that God is able to step in and use our situation for his glory. When thoughts race through your mind and you hit a wall that feels impossible for you to climb, this is when it's important to remind ourselves of what **Mark 10:27 ESV** states: "With man it is impossible, but not with God. For all things are possible with God." He is trying to tell you that no matter how hard you try on your own, these challenges in life are going to be hard to overcome on your own strength. However, when I prayed for a breakthrough, I was not realizing that God had given me everything that I needed internally. Sometimes, I thought my breakthrough and the opportunities I sought would come from man. I had to come face-to-face with the reality that God was talking to me and I had no choice but to listen. See, so many times we do one million tasks hoping that things will work out the way we want them to. We try to do everything possible to make things go our way in life. You may be at your breaking point, but I came to tell you today that it is at your breaking point that God can remold you, restructure you, and reform you. Only he can break you down and put you back together. What I've learned is that your broken place is where you need a breakthrough. Sometimes, you don't just need a breakthrough, you need God to break you and put you back together to give you a fresh new start in life. It wasn't until I was all out of options that I fell to my knees, and asked God for help after going for years on my own train.

CHAPTER 8
It's Supernatural

When I look back over my life, I see that God has always performed supernatural blessings over me. I think about my youth and the times growing up, and some of the stories that were told to me about my childbirth. I was born with challenges and the doctor said there wasn't a chance I would live. My kidney collapsed in 1977. Technology wasn't what it is in this day and age. However, God is the author and the creator of all things and his power has the ability to override any medical man-made technology. My mother, who was a young mom, went into the other room, locked the door and began to pray. She looked up to God and asked him to keep me. She said, "Lord, if you keep my son, I promise I will take care of him. I will support him, and I will always be by his side." God is not limited by time, so it did not matter if the doctors understood or had the ability to fix the problem. My mother had called on the creator, and she tapped into God's supernatural power and by his spirit I was healed. He allowed me to make it through the surgery and live a healthy life. This was my introduction, at an early age of just a few days old, to God's amazing power. Only he could have intervened and put a blessing over my life because he heard my mother's prayers.

I also remember a time when I was a kid and school got out early. My mom was at work, and she thought my aunt had picked me up, only to find out that she hadn't. I was left outside the elementary school. As a little boy standing on the corner looking around for my mom for hours, I went into a panic, not knowing where I was. My mother called on the Lord to protect me. She found me hiding in a corner on the far-right side of the school building. Fortunately, I was safe and no one had harmed me. However, I went to school in a rough community that had high crime rates, along with a lot of drugs and suspicious people in the area. For hours, I once again experienced God's amazing power. It was his supernatural power and angels that protected me. God had again watched over me in my time of need.

Another time, in my teenage years, I was walking around the corner to the neighborhood we once lived in. Two guys got out of a car, armed and ready to pull the trigger as I was walking. When I looked at the guy, he looked at me, then the other guy reached in his jacket, looking me in the eyes. Staring at him, he said, "No that's not him," and got back in the car. It scared me, but in that moment, I believe those guys saw the angels around me. Before they were sure that I was someone else. There are many people who have been murdered for mistaken identity, but I believe God supernaturally stepped in and allowed his angels to ensure that these guys recognized me and saw that I was not who they were looking for.

I remember a time my oldest sister and I were sleeping when we were about ten years old. I opened my eyes and saw an angel. It looked like a female with a gold crown and gold hair. I could not quite see her face, but her face was so bright that it looked like gold. I remember seeing her face for at least a minute or two, then it vanished. I believe that was God letting me see into the spiritual realm and letting me know that he would be present throughout my entire life.

I've had so many challenges and wild experiences; I guess the devil knew this promise to me as well. For years of my life, he tried to fight and block me from walking in my purpose and getting close to God. He had already laid out everything for me from day one of my life. At the age of sixteen years old, I was in a dance group, creating music and dancing. It was really my passion. I loved it, but deep down inside me, I always felt an emptiness. When I was doing music and could talk about God's word to a friend, I would get a hold of a Bible to feel safe and complete. I felt a sense of purpose even at a young age; I was always interested in God's word, and I just could not understand why.

I remember the first time picking up the Bible and reading the book of Revelations. It was amazing to me. I remember the first time I read Genesis, I was blown away and began to understand how life was created and more about the creation of this world that we live in. It was so exciting and I could not put it down. It was almost like I had finally found my life. However, once I began to experience life, I started to get further and further away from what it was that God planned for me from day one. I got into the music business, started traveling as a Motown artist, meeting all of these people, then started to drift far away from my purpose. Yet, God clearly states that what the enemy tries to use for bad, God can use for your good. **Genesis 50:20 NIV**: "You intended to harm me, but God intended it for good to accomplish what is now being done, the saving of many lives." If I had not become a recording artist and experienced some of those things, I would not have been able to share some of the testimonies and God's faithfulness that I've shared in previous books. In those times where he was definitely needed, I started to focus on me being the savior to my family. I thought I had to become rich to try to escape our problems, but in the back of my mind, I knew the only way we would have a better life is by realigning back with God in the same way it was when

I was first born. I endured so many spiritual battles and attacks that the enemy was really working hard on me in more ways than one. It was a challenge and was not easy. I knew the enemy had made a commitment to try to stop me from getting access to what it was that God had already had for me over many years. I felt like I was wandering in the wilderness, lost, running around in circles. The whole time God was there to do what he had been doing my whole life; using his supernatural power to protect me and bless me. Yet, I could not see it at times because I thought that it was all about me. I thought all of the great things that had happened in my life were because of me. Yes God had blessed me, but there was so much more he had in store for me, he was just waiting on me to totally submit, focus, and walk with him. I understand that he had already written out a plan for my life.

When we have uncertain times, it's very important that you take a moment to reflect on the past blessings in your life. Sometimes, when you're going through certain ups and downs in life, we tend to get lost in that moment, forgetting about past blessings and God's faithfulness throughout our lives. Once we hit that wall, it's almost like we become totally absent-minded to the things that God has done over and over in our life. He has been performing supernatural blessings your entire life. Just think about how many times in your life that you had no clue why you were experiencing some of the things you were experiencing. When you look back, you go *Wow I can't believe that I not only made it through this situation, but it worked out for my good.* Then you begin to be grateful for that experience. **Jeremiah 1:5 NIV,** "Before I formed you in the womb I knew you, before you were born I set you apart; I appointed you as prophets to the nations." Reading this Bible verse gives confirmation and has helped me remember that God knows everything about us; he knows when we're going to hit a wall, and when we're headed down the wrong road. Still, he always rescues us. He just waits for us to slow down and let him be God.

The enemy thrives off your lack of cooperation with God. The less you cooperate, the more power you give the enemy. The devil loves when the person who has a calling in their life gets out of line with God. This is because, in that space, you are disconnected from your creator, making it easy for the enemy to tamper with you and send you off into the wandering, dry desert. That's why it's so important during those challenging and uncertain times to remember that God has it all worked out in the situation that you're in now. All you have to do is change your perspective and really take a look at the situation you're in, then ask yourself, "Is this really a totally bad situation, or am I still holding on to my selfish wants, needs, and desires?" It's just like the person who lost a job, and felt like it was the end of the world because they did not want to let go even though God had better plans for them. He saw the frustration and disappointment in your heart after you lost a job, and he also saw all of your trust and everything you've put into the situation dwindle away. But if only you would just be OK with not being in control, and be OK with whatever it is that God has for you next. When we're in that dark, broken, disappointed place, sometimes you just have to let it go and ask God what his plan is for you, then be OK with his plan.

Your prayers are more powerful than you know

Philippians 4:6-7 NKJV, states "Be anxious for nothing but in everything by **prayer** and **supplication**, with thanksgiving, let your request be made known to God, and the peace of God which surpasses all understanding, will guard your hearts and minds through Christ Jesus." We see that God gives us access to him no matter what your trial may be. No matter what you may be going through, he gives us direct access through prayer. At some point, we have to start looking at prayer as a conversation and not some mysterious act. Think about this: when you talk with your earthly parents, you see them as someone that you have a personal relationship with; that's kind of how God wants us to see him. Unfortunately, a lot of us find it hard to see God as a father, and think we have to come to having some special prayer skill without knowing exactly what to say or the perfect speech.

It's not about knowing every single Bible scripture word for word or line for line. We have to start looking at God for who he is: the creator. He is our heavenly Father; he knows everything about us. His love cannot be compared to any other. We have to start coming to him and trusting that he hears our prayers; that is our communication to the heavenly Father that is life-changing. It took me years to really understand this. There would be times when I would talk to God and I honestly would not expect him to do everything that I prayed for. It was because I still saw him as a distant relationship, so it took more work, reading and studying before I started to see him as a personal father. You may even be reading this book and also find your relationship with God hard. You may not see him as someone that is close to you. Instead, you may just simply see him as this powerful being that is untouchable to man. I'm telling you he is closer to you than you think. Let's recall the many nights where I had to just call on his name, and I honestly didn't know if he would hear my prayers. I always wondered why God would want to listen to me, or just did not know what exactly to say. I just believed in him without fully knowing if he would really respond to my prayers. Many Bible verses tell us that God is near to us and waiting for us to call on him. **Matthew 11:28 ESV**: "Come to me, all who labor and are heavy laden, and I will give you rest." **James 4:8 ESV**: "Draw near to God, and he will draw near to you." **Romans 10:13 ESV**: "For everyone who calls on the name of the lord will be saved."

CHAPTER 9
Spiritual Fitness

It takes more than just faith to get through your storms. It takes work and being spiritually fit to stand the test of time. Many people talk about working out every day, but little do they know your faith works the same way. Just like in physical fitness, if you don't use your muscles, they get weak. It's the same thing with your faith. If you don't practice it every day, if you don't build it, don't read, don't meditate on the word, don't pray or take in the word on a daily basis, your spiritual muscles will also get weak. When your spiritual muscles get weak, you become extremely vulnerable and won't have the ability to fight a good fight because you are spiritually out of shape. You may be physically strong, but have you ever wondered how a person can be in top shape with a six pack, strong arms, legs, chest, but spiritually they are nowhere near developed? It's because their spiritual muscles have been starved for so long, that they've lost their strength and ability to fight back during times of trial. In this chapter, I have put together a spiritual fitness plan to help you.

Following these directions will help you get spiritually fit:

1. Read.

2. Make time for prayer daily.

3. Before you get out the bed, thank God for another day and give the day to him.

4. Take time to reflect on all the blessings you have in your life, down to the smallest.

5. Remember and learn four scriptures every month.

6. Have a day that's totally devoted to God, even if it's just for a few hours.

7. Before you sleep, talk with God.

8. Manage the amount of news you take in.

9. Get plenty of rest.

10. Before you make any major decision, pray it will help avoid unnecessary problems.

11. Meditate on God's word daily.

12. Be cautious of what you take in on television and your cell phone.

13. Download Bible apps.

14. When taking a morning walk or run, listen to inspirational music or the word.

Next, I want you to repeat these scriptures on a daily basis:

- God is faithful; he will not let you be tempted beyond what you can bear. But when you are tempted, he will also provide a way out so that you can endure it. **(1 Corinthians 10:13 NIV)**

- Be anxious for nothing, but in everything by prayer and supplication, with thanksgiving, let your requests be made known to God; and the peace of God, which surpasses all understanding, will guard your hearts and minds through Christ Jesus. **(Philippians 4:6-7 NKJV)**

- For God hath not given us the spirit of fear; but of power, and of love, and of a sound mind. **(2 Timothy 1:7 KJV)**

- For the Lord your God is he who goes with you to fight for you against your enemies, to give you victory. **(Deuteronomy 20:4 ESV)**

- What, then, shall we say in response to these things? If God is for us, who can be against us? (**Romans 8:31 NIV**)

- Have I not commanded you? Be strong and courageous. Do not be afraid; do not be discouraged, for the Lord your God will be with you wherever you go. (**Joshua 1:9 NIV**)

- Yet those who wait for the Lord will gain new strength; they will mount up with wings like eagles, they will run and not get tired, they will walk and not become weary. (**Isaiah 40:31 NASB**)

- Give all your worries and cares to God, for he cares about you. (**1 Peter 5:7 NLT**)

- You will keep him in perfect peace, whose mind is stayed on You, because he trusts in You. (**Isaiah 26:3 NKJV**)

Now that you've read these scriptures, you've already worked on spiritual fitness. Remember this: God is always working, but because you're out of shape spiritually, you probably won't be able to see it. That's why spiritual fitness is very important. I'm just so happy you made a decision to get spiritually fit, because God is always working things out for your good. He is maneuvering things around in the background and repositioning things while you're going through this moment. He's setting you up for something great. He's working on the hearts of the people around you. Maybe he's giving your enemies a change of heart; maybe he's working on some of your delayed prayers. Regardless, God is working even when you think he's not. Maybe someone betrayed you: he could be working on the person who let you down. Maybe he's holding things up, so that you can let some of the people who you've been looking up to go before you, so you can watch them to know which way you should not go. Maybe he's showing you that the ways you think are right could lead to disaster and put you in a bad position. Just because you feel that you're not where you want to be, it does not mean that you are lost. Sometimes, God allows you to stay back so that you can work on yourself and become spiritually fit. That way, when he moves you up, you're ready for that kind of capacity in your life. I think back on how many times I was in challenging situations, and I could not see what was really going on around me. It's important to be spiritually grounded, so that life doesn't become tricky.

We all go through different trials in life and should adjust to the altitude as we climb higher in our walk with God. The problem is that people go their entire life operating on the same system they were running off of years ago. It's just like a cell phone, each time you're alerted to update your phone so that the device functions properly. This happens so you can maximize all of the features on the phone. It's the same system from a spiritual perspective when God wants us to upgrade ourselves. He wants us to improve our spiritual operating system on a daily basis. You're then more prepared for those challenging times when you have worked on yourself regularly. This will put you in a position to come out of any uncertain moment in your life holding your head up high because you are spiritually fit.

CHAPTER 10
Why We Struggle So Hard When it Comes to Relying on God

One day, I was talking to a friend, and we spoke about a newborn baby and faith. I told my homeboy about how my son relies on my wife's breasts to eat, and how God created him to rely on her breasts to feed. To my son, his mother is his whole entire world. She feeds him, nurtures him, and is a place of safety for him. God designed it to be that way without him even knowing why. He just knows this is how God created it, and knows it's a natural thing without any second thoughts. Just like when Adam and Eve were in the garden, we relied on God, because that's all we knew in that moment. He gave us everything we needed in that garden. We did not know there were other options outside of relying on God. Yet, the Bible says once we ate from the tree of life, we knew good from evil. From that point on, we felt like we had other options outside of God.

You see, it's just like politics. People say, "OK, we know God created all things; however, we need these men to help make things better." As we go through life, we get introduced to all of these things outside of God, then end up putting our trust in one thing after the next. Just think back to what I said about when Adam and Eve ate from the tree. They no longer saw God as their provider. They no longer saw him as their place of comfort, security and joy. After they sinned, they gained the ability to pick and choose good from evil based on their own free will.

Unfortunately, we have gotten so far away from the creator that it seems as if we are too far gone. In **Psalms 34:18 ESV**, it is written that, "The Lord is near to the brokenhearted and saves the crushed in spirit." I always understood this scripture as saying that, no matter how far away from God we get or feel, he is still present even in our brokenness. He is waiting for us to call on him and seek him for direction. Even if it's our twentieth time trying to do things on our own, or we keep hitting our head against the wall, we should still get on our knees and pray to him; he will open his arms.

CHAPTER 11
Your First Hurt: I Can Never Catch a Break

While life throws different blows at us, have you ever sat back and thought about how unpredictable life can be? Sometimes, it's so impulsive, especially when we keep experiencing the same kinds of problems over and over again. Have you ever wondered why it seems like your whole entire life keeps producing the same problem? Sometimes, it feels like it will never stop. One thing you may not have thought of is that one of the reasons you keep hitting the same walls is because your decisions are reflecting your past hurt and early experiences in your life. "For we wrestle not against flesh and blood, but against principalities, against powers, against the rulers of the darkness of this world, against spiritual wickedness in high places." (**Ephesians 6:12 KJV**)

The foundation

Your first hurt is what the enemy banks on, so he comes up with ways to cause your first hurt to build a foundation or a playground on. In the dictionary, the word "hurt" is defined as meaning "to cause physical damage or pain; to cause mental or emotional suffering; to distress; to cause harm." The enemy banks on your first encounter with hurt because he knows you are anointed. You have something special inside you and he knows it. He finds a way very early on in life to tamper with you, which is why many gifted and amazing people go through so much as children. He immediately comes in to interfere. This may take the form of people being harmed by their own family members, even their own father or mother. Some have even been let down by a pastor they admired. Satan banks on that first hurt, that first emotional distress, that first physical damage, anything that will hurt you or alter your calling in life. Remember, he knows that you have a light over you, so he hates you for that. In times like this, remember **Genesis 50:20 NIV:** "you intended to harm me, but God intended it for good to accomplish what is now being done, the saving of many lives." He loves to work through your faith after your first major hurt.

Satan goes through your entire life playing mind games based on the one experience that hurt you. Let's take a closer look at how he accomplished this. It could be when you were married and your spouse hurt you. After the marriage, you moved on to the next person with fear and worry because you were still living in the past of what happened to you. Before you even got into the new relationship that you are currently in, he knew that for your entire life you had looked forward to having a happy marriage, family, and a home. He knows your goals are to spend the rest of your life with this person. Thus, he was able to get in and destroy your entire world from that moment. From this point on, your life would never be the same.

Another example: As a child, your mom or dad called you fat or other things to hurt you, so you spent your whole entire life trying to find a way to lose weight and stay small. Spending your whole life looking for approval from others, you were constantly let down and felt you were never good enough for anyone. The enemy knows that one moment in your life could create a lifelong journey of trying to find the love and affection you never experience. So, he uses those hurtful experiences against you. Whatever it is that hurt you the first time is what Satan uses to build a foundation of hurt throughout your life. That is why it's so hard for many people to get over that early pain. Satan knows it's very hard to repair those hurts. He knows that it will take a lot of work to fix or recover from that hurt.

The good news I want to tell you today is that we serve a God that is loving. We serve a God that is merciful and can do all things. We serve a God that can make possible even those things that we think are impossible. I give the glory to God, for he is faithful and is in control of all things. I thank the Lord because, had it not been for his mercy and his love, we all would be destroyed. We would not be able to heal and get past the first hurt. We would be living a life trapped by past experiences, but we aren't, because God gave us his word.

The Bible says we must come into a renewal of the mind. God gave us these scriptures to live by as food for the broken mind, the broken soul, the broken spirit. He doesn't want us to live off feelings, only off the word of God. For as a man thinks in his heart, so is he. (Proverbs 23:7) We are up against the enemy who does not have a heart for mankind. It's just like when a father walks out on his family or a woman walks away from her family, the kids get hurt. Satan immediately comes in and starts to water that hurt. That child turns into an adult chasing after love their whole life, because what they loved was taken away from them. Satan toys with that and will send demons of bad relationships to play off of the fact that you chase love in all the wrong places. So, he puts tricks in front of people who chase love, he put all kinds of things in front of broken-hearted people to control you. This leads to more damage and disappointment. The hurt can bring you to a place where you are so low that you do not even want to live anymore. **John 10:10-29 NIV** states: "The thief comes only to steal and kill and destroy." No matter what age you are—one or fifty-one, or ninety-one—Satan waits to water your hurt or look for an opportunity to cause hurt. Major changes in life do not matter, because he will try to water the pain. At the end of the day, remember Satan waters your hurt. However, it's up to God for it to grow. As **1 Corinthians 3:7 ESV** states: "So neither he who plants nor he who waters is anything, but only God who gives the growth."

The host

The devil is just like a virus who needs a host to enter into; that host is usually a person you would least expect it to be. The enemy is a spirit, and spirit creatures need a body to manipulate. Have you ever been around someone who is so negative you can feel the energy? Their whole presence is very dark. You may come to them with some great news, full of joy, and this person does nothing but talk down on everything you come to them with. Most of the time, Satan loves that person to be someone you love and care about or look up to. Through that person, he can make your life horrible because this is someone who your heart is connected to. The Bible says where your heart is, there your treasures lie. God wants us to give him our full heart so that the enemy will have less power over us.

Do you ever wonder why most people have experienced so much childhood trauma from their own family? Think about this: the family is one of the most precious things to God, and the enemy knows this, so if he can try to break the family, he knows that this will impact not only your family and home, but also society and your future. Whether it's your future husband or wife, even coworkers or friends, he knows that people who are broken will hurt those around them. In doing so, he creates a never-ending vicious cycle of hurt and pain. In order to destroy your growth, he must attack your root. By attacking the root, you cause the growth of a person to be redirected. Satan's focus is to block you from getting to your God-given calling in your life. He knows the gift you have over your life. If used for God's glory, it will bring many people to Christ. That's why we have so many amazing people in very dark places like jail and on drugs, making them want to give up on themselves. Somewhere in life the gift and ability that God planted inside of them never got used the right way. Many people throughout their lives fell for Satan's tactics, trying to convince them that they are worthless and that God doesn't love them. Because of the hurt they went through, they started to believe that God never hears their prayers. Some people convinced themselves that their life will never be better. Some even believe that it's just life and it will forever be this way. However, according to the Bible, the devil is a liar. **Romans 8:31 NIV** states: "If God is for us, who can be against us"? Before we move forward with this book, understand that no matter what the enemy has done in your life, no matter how hurtful and frustrating the experience, God is still able to heal you and turn your negative life around. He can bless someone else. This is what the enemy really hates: when a person's life is negative for so long, and then that person turns their life around to bless others.

CHAPTER 12
Seeing Through Appearances

One of the greatest wisdoms is seeing through appearances, and finding the true gift from God. In times of confusion, how many times have we passed up gifts that were put in front of us from God and, because it did not match human expectations, we looked right past it? This chapter will make you think about things and their appearances very differently. When help comes, you will be able to see clearly in dark times what's from God and what's not from God.

Now let's learn how to receive your gift

Seek first God's kingdom, and be ready for the task God may give you that comes along with the gift. Things aren't always what they seem. Satan's gifts are all about the outside; God's gift focuses on the inside of man. Most of the time, Satan's gifts look better than God's gifts, because he just wants you to open the gift. Satan's gifts are death traps; they will deceive you. **2 Corinthians 5:7 ESV** states: "For we walk by faith, not by sight." God's gifts bring life, joy, completion, happiness and understanding. In uncertain times, remember that Satan doesn't want you to live by faith, he wants you to live by sight. Don't be deceived when he approaches you in those moments of doubt. Remember, his gifts may look good, but they bring pain, depression, confusion and hurt. You have to be very careful in that moment not to make decisions that will cause long-term damage and affect your life. I know you may be desperate and tired or frustrated, but be patient and wait on the Lord. In this season, you will have a lot of things to come your way and they will look pretty on the outside, but trust me when I tell you it won't be worth it. You have to be very careful in that moment not to make decisions that will have long-term damage and affect your life.

The enemy thrives when you are in a confused, uncertain and broken space. This is where he plays hardball. He pulls all of his weapons out to use everything in his power to keep you in the space of confusion and blindness. You will be introduced to many things. There will be people who will have you believe that they're giving you a gift and inviting you into their world, but be careful in this season. Not all gifts are good, and not all gifts are from God.

Jesus was a gift and he came on a donkey. **John 12:12-19** talks about Jesus' triumphant entry into Jerusalem. Jesus did not ride into Jerusalem on a horse as warrior king, but entered on a donkey in gentleness and peace to give salvation. Jesus didn't come looking outwardly impressive, and yet he was the greatest man who ever lived. Jesus' death was the greatest gift to humankind.

Let's look deeper: what is a gift? An object given without the expectation of payment. God is the Father of giving loving gifts and he expects no repayment. God picks what gift you should have based on the calling for your life after you seek him first. Remember, in the beginning, Satan used what God had given Adam as a gift to deceive him. That's why once we receive godly wisdom, we are able to make sound decisions. Wisdom is the quality or state of being wise, and having knowledge of what is true or right. God gives you these three abilities when you seek him first: discernment, insight, just judgment. Discernment is the ability to judge well. Insight is the capacity to discern the true nature of a situation. Just judgment involves acting or being in conformity with what is normally considered upright or good. Never forget: sight may refer to visual perception—something that is seen. Once you seek God first, no matter what your situation may be, no matter what you may be going through, you will be able to see things more clearly. At times Satan's gifts are all based on selfishness.

They are for you to have bad vision when you walk with the Devil and not God. All God wants you to do is seek his ways, but Satan toys with your mind all day to stop this. He presents all of these options to you, trying to distract you from receiving your blessing in the storm. He's hoping that he can rob you of the gift that God wants to build in your darkest times, because this is when you are faced with obstacles that will question your faith and ability to stay strong. In these moments, when you're up against the wall, you're forced to practice your faith. The deeper you dig, the closer you get to your gift, and it is your gift that God has already given you that will set you free.

CHAPTER 13
The Waiting Season

How many times in your life have you wanted something so bad that it got put on hold? How many times did you anticipate a big moment in your life, and the time that you thought it would take place, it ended up getting pushed back, making you more and more anxious for it to come? In this season of your life, you will have to wait on God. It may not feel right to you, but God's time is always on time. In this season of waiting, this is the time for you to practice patience. I remember years ago, it was thundering and lightning so bad in my mind. I was walking around with an umbrella and it was not even raining outside. Yet, there was hell going on in my mind, and it started to show on the outside of me. When I realized I was doing too much thinking, I could make things move faster. Little did I know, God had other plans for me, just not on my time. Ask yourself: how many times have you tried to play God and control the outcome or season of your blessings? Here are some Bible verses to teach you how to wait on God and the benefit of waiting on the Lord. Please read them: they will bless you in the long seasons of waiting for your breakthrough. Remember, God's word never changes.

Jesus promised us in John 16:33 KJV, "These things I have spoken unto you, that in me ye might have peace. In the world ye shall have tribulation: but be of good cheer; I have overcome the world." God is with us in every season of our life.

Ecclesiastes 3:1-5 ESV: "For everything there is a season, and a time for every matter under heaven: a time to be born, and a time to die; a time to plant, and a time to pluck up what is planted; a time to kill, and a time to heal; a time to break down, and a time to build up; a time to weep, and a time to laugh; a time to mourn, and a time to dance; a time to cast away stones, and a time to gather stones together; a time to embrace, and a time to refrain from embracing."

Acts 1:7 ESV: "He said to them, "It is not for you to know times or seasons that the father has fixed by his own authority.""

James 1:12 ESV: "Blessed is the man who remains steadfast under trial, for when he has stood the test he will receive the crown of life, which God has promised to those who love him."

2 Peter 3:8 ESV: "But do not overlook this one fact, beloved, that with the Lord one day is as a thousand years, and a thousand years as one day."

Daniel 2:21 ESV: "He changes times and seasons; he removes kings and sets up kings; he gives wisdom to the wise and knowledge to those who have understanding."

Habakkuk 2:3 ESV: "For still the vision awaits its appointed time; it hastens to the end—it will not lie. If it seems slow, wait for it; it will surely come; it will not delay."

After reading these scriptures, wait on God and pray that you will understand how much in control God is in all of these seasons. In those moments, stand still and trust that God will show up on time. "The mind of man plans his way, but the Lord directs his steps" **Proverbs 16:9 NASB**. For our purposes this is something of a companion piece to **Proverbs 3:5-6**. No matter what kind of planning you commit to or how tough your work ethic, things don't always go according to plan. Trust in God more than you believe in your own plans.

CHAPTER 14
Double Life

We live in two worlds: the one people can see, and the one in the mind that no one can see. We live in a visual world, yet all damage, pain, hurt and war lives and comes from within the mind. The emotions drive most action in the world, yet the mind is the most hidden weapon and power on the face of the planet. The mind has the ability to create and solve problems. The mind has the ability to change one's life and start a war. The mind has healing powers, yet we live in a world that focuses less on the mind. We focus on external things for the most part. This is why most people live a real double life. To some extent, we all live a double life. The mind can be its worst enemy or its best blessing. The Bible says that it's with the mind that we serve the Lord (Romans 7:25). **Romans 12:2a NIV**: "Do not conform to the pattern of this world, but be transformed by the renewing of your mind." Any problem can be fixed by the word of God. We spend so much money trying to find an answer and for the most part people keep trying to live without God, when he is roadmap and the word feeds the mind. Unfortunately, we only care about and take care of what we see.

CHAPTER 15

Scriptures to Remember in Difficult Times

When you face different obstacles, you will need to put on the full armor of God. I have listed ten scriptures below for you to remember at all times no matter what. These scriptures will save you, bless you and protect you in storms and times of confusion.

Isaiah 41:10 NIV: "So do not fear, for I am with you; do not be dismayed, for I am your God. I will strengthen you and help you; I will uphold you with my righteous right hand."

Joshua 1:9 ESV: "Be strong and courageous. Do not be frightened, and do not be dismayed, for the Lord your God is with you wherever you go."

Isaiah 40:29 NLT: "He gives power to weak and strength to the powerless."

Philippians 4:13 NIV: "I can do all this through him who gives me strength."

2 Thessalonians 3:3 NIV: "But the Lord is faithful, and he will strengthen you and protect you from the evil one."

Proverbs 3:5-6 NIV: "Trust in the Lord with all your heart and lean not on your own understanding; in all your ways submit to him, and he will make your paths straight."

Philippians 4:6-7 NIV: "Do not be anxious about anything, but in every situation, by prayer and petition, with thanksgiving, present your requests to God. And the peace of god which transcends all understanding, will guard your hearts and your minds in Christ Jesus."

Psalm 23:4 NIV: "Even though I walk through the darkest valley, I will fear no evil, for you are with me; your rod and your staff, they comfort me."

John 20:29 ESV: "Jesus said to him, "Have you believed because you have seen me? Blessed are those who have not seen and yet have believed.""

Philippians 4:12-13 NIV: "I know what it is to be in need, and I know what it is to have plenty. I have learned the secret of being content in any and every situation, and whether well fed or hungry, whether living in plenty or in want. I can do all this through him who gives me strength."

Deuteronomy 31:6 NKJV: "Be strong and of good courage, do not fear nor be afraid of them; for the Lord your God, He is the One who goes with you. He will not leave you nor forsake you."

Psalm 91 NIV: Whoever dwells in the shelter of the Most High will rest in the shadow of the Almighty. I will say of the Lord, "He is my refuge and my fortress, my God, in whom I trust." Surely he will save you from the fowler's snare and from the deadly pestilence. He will cover you with his feathers, and under his wings you will find refuge; his faithfulness will be your shield and rampart. You will not fear the terror of night, nor the arrow that flies by day, nor the pestilence that stalks in the darkness, nor the plague that destroys at midday. A thousand may fall at your side, ten thousand at your right hand, but it will not come near you. You will only observe with your eyes and see the punishment of the wicked. If you say, "The Lord is my refuge," and you make the Most High your dwelling, no harm will overtake you, no disaster will come near your tent. For he will command his angels concerning you to guard you in all your ways; they will lift you up in their hands, so that you will not strike your foot against a stone. You will tread on the lion and the cobra; you will trample the great lion and the serpent.

"Because he loves me," says the Lord, "I will rescue him; I will protect him, for he acknowledges my name. He will call on me, and I will answer him;

I will be with him in trouble, I will deliver him and honor him. With long life I will satisfy him and show him my salvation.

John 16:33 NIV: "In this world you will have trouble. But take heart! I have overcome the world."

CHAPTER 16

Why Worry?

Your emotions follow your devotions, we worry about the things we are most devoted to. **Matthew 6:24 NIV:** "No one can serve two masters. Either you will hate the one and love the other, or you will be devoted to the one and despise the other. You cannot serve both God and money."

Matthew 6:25- 34 NIV: "Therefore I tell you, do not worry about your life, what you will eat or drink; or about your body, what you will wear. Is not life more than food, and the body more than clothes? Look at the birds of the air; they do not sow or reap or store away in barns, and yet your heavenly Father feeds them. Are you not much more valuable than they? Can any one of you by worrying add a single hour to your life? And why do you worry about clothes? See how the flowers of the field grow. They do not labor or spin. Yet I tell you that not even Solomon in all his splendor was dressed like one of these. If that is how

God clothes the grass of the field, which is here today and tomorrow is thrown into the fire, will he not much more clothe you—you of little faith? So do not worry, saying, 'What shall we eat?' or 'What shall we drink?' or 'What shall we wear?' For the pagans run after all these things, and your heavenly Father knows that you need them. But seek first his kingdom and his righteousness, and all these things will be given to you as well. Therefore do not worry about tomorrow, for tomorrow will worry about itself. Each day has enough trouble of its own."

I put these scriptures in here because like myself and many others in uncertain times, we constantly turn to ourselves and tend to fall back on the old patterns of behavior every time we get into a jam. When times of uncertainty come to our table, we for some reason repeat the same actions over and over again hoping that things will turn out differently. We don't realize that it will not turn out differently because once again we're relying on self. You're taking more on then you need to; you're worrying yourself. I know it is easier said than done, but throughout my life I've learned many lessons from allowing myself to worry and taking on unnecessary stress in my life. Have you ever thought about when sometimes things happen, people say it's the devil? Sometimes, God will allow us to experience uncertain times, maybe to humble us a little bit and get to the core of who we truly are. Sometimes, it's so we can be molded and be re-created and rebuilt to be used for his purpose. Someone once said, "No pressure, no diamonds." Sometimes, in order for you to become the better version of yourself, you have to go through some crushing to break you all the way down. You can build all the way back up to be made beautifully.

CHAPTER 17
The Next Chapter

Everyone has the next chapter. Sometimes, the only way you can get there is through a storm. That's the part that separates so many people. Unfortunately, people get stuck in chapters, not because they want to be stuck in the chapter. Many times, we think in order to get to the next phase in life, the transition will be easy. Some people actually have the ability to naturally transition well, but most of us don't. Let's talk about what could be some of the challenges in that transition and how faith plays a major part in that transition. In that space, when you're going towards the next chapter, the page has to be turned. Depending on how heavy, how much baggage, how many problems and unresolved issues in that chapter will determine how much strength is needed to turn to that chapter of your life. That's where faith steps in. I lived this and it's real; moving on or starting over or letting the past be the past is tough. You have to walk forward and not look back at everything that's happened when you take the first step out on faith. You can't look back to the old chapter of your life.

Life is so interesting because you don't know what's ahead of you. Not knowing what lies on the other side can be very frightening in uncertain times. It's easier to stay stuck in familiar territory, rather than moving forward in unfamiliar territory. Because we don't know what the outcome will be, we allow ourselves to become a victim of that moment in your life. You know in your heart it's time to move on, however, the problem is you keep trying to do it on your own! Every time you get in a jam, in your mind you have convinced yourself that only you can set yourself free. For years, you stay in the same place and are continuously unable to move forward and explore new possibilities in your life.

Proverbs 3:5-6 NIV: "Trust in the LORD with all your heart and lean not on your own understanding; in all your ways submit to him, and he will make your paths straight."

2 Corinthians 5:17 KJV: "Therefore if any man be in Christ, he is a new creature: old things are passed away; behold, all things are become new."

EZEKIEL 11:19-20 KJV: "And I will give them one heart, and I will put a new spirit within you; and I will take the stoney heart out of their flesh, and will give them an heart of flesh: that they may walk in my statutes, and keep mine ordinances, and do them: and they shall be my people, and I will be their God."

At one of their darkest hours, God promised the Israelites He would bring them back home to the land. He bequeathed to them many years before. The purpose of this was not only to make them happier or healthier, but to bring them closer to Him. Know that no matter where you are starting over from, he is able to draw you near and make you whole. He will replace your heart of stone with one of flesh.

Colossians 3:17 NIV "And whatever you do, whether in word or deed, do it all in the name of the Lord Jesus, giving thanks to God the Father through him."

Starting over can sound appealing to us for many reasons, but we must remember that no matter what we do, all is to be done for the glory of God. That's just as true for the mom who's looking to get more organized as it is for the middle-aged man who is looking to launch his own company. We can always reinvent ourselves and proclaim the name of Jesus in the process.

(K-LOVE Fan Awards – fanawards.com/ motivational-bible-verses-about-starting-over)

Remember just because a transition is difficult doesn't mean we're outside of God's will. What's for you will be for you at its perfect time. Never give up no matter how hard change is in your life, you can do it because you've got God on your side.

CHAPTER 18

Why Me Lord?

How many times have you asked yourself this question? How many times have you thought this to yourself? How many times have you laid in bed looking up at the ceiling and said this to yourself? How many times have you said this phrase when things got rough? Most of us have. In uncertain times and challenging times, it's really hard, so we sometimes question God because in that moment we feel isolated and alone. We feel that the world has come crashing down on us with no way out. This is where your faith will be tested. In this moment, you will really need to trust and understand biblical scripture, because when we hit the wall, that's when we feel like we're the only ones in the world who are dealing with the situation. That's how the enemy wants you to see it. I'm not a professional or a medical doctor to give my opinion on mental health. However, when I look at suicide, I wonder to myself what thoughts must have been going through someone's mind in that dark moment of their life. As I gained spiritual wisdom, I realized that there is a medical and spiritual part to this. Medically speaking, many people suffer from chemical imbalances and other mental challenges. On a day to day basis, they may be faced with many challenges in their mind. Trust me, I have had personal experiences. However, even those who may not suffer from mental issues, in hard times are attacked by the enemy with negative thoughts. These could include thoughts of hopelessness, thoughts of fear, thoughts of worry, thoughts of doubt, thoughts of loneliness, and thoughts of pain. Remember, thoughts trigger feelings and emotions of depression. I'm sure we all have questioned ourselves, wondering whether we did something wrong to deserve this punishment. What could I have done to be put through so much? The reality is what you are experiencing may have nothing to do with how you see yourself, how you feel about yourself and what you have done. Let's take a look at the scripture, **Nehemiah 8:10** b, **NIV:** "Do not grieve, for the joy of the Lord is your strength." **Isaiah 41:10, NIV:** "So do not fear, for I am with you; do not be dismayed, for I am your God. I will strengthen you and help you; I will uphold you with my righteous right hand."

Sometimes, it's just a test and God allows us to endure many things to bring glory to his name in the end. I guess the challenge is remembering the scriptures and God's promises, and leaning not on your own opinion of the trials that you may be facing. If we could just trust God in this moment and rest on his word, maybe your question of, "Why me, Lord" would become clear. **Romans 8:28, NIV:** "And we know that in all things God works for the good of those who love him, who have been called according to his purpose."

So I advise you in your craziest moments to turn to the word before you call your friends to talk to anyone. Turn to the word no matter what you're going through. We see according to God's word that he has a plan for you, and it may not seem like it today or even tomorrow, but in his perfect time he will make everything that you're going through make sense when you look back at that time and place of your life. Sadly, so many people have these tough times and they give up. They don't see any type of help; they unfortunately drown in their misery and negative thoughts in pain. I'm not saying that this is easy, but what I am saying is it's worth giving it one more try before you give up and turn to God's word. You won't always understand life from a spiritual perspective, but when your eyes become open in the challenges that you're going through, the hard times that will appear different. Make a decision to reach out and call on the creator for help. I'm not saying you should not seek professional medical help at all. I am saying that some things we go through in life are much deeper than we know, so we need to make sure that we have taken the necessary medical steps and, more importantly, the spiritual steps needed to understand in order to get through the roadblocks in your life.

CHAPTER 19

God's Favor

Favor from God is something that is impossible to understand with our own human understanding. God favors his people. One of the hardest parts is understanding how he favors his people. When he shows favor to his people, most of the time it's during the most challenging and craziest times of our lives. When people are looking at us and saying, "There is no way you can do this during this time." How do you open a business when the economy is collapsing? How do you buy a home with millions of Americans losing their jobs? How did you become more successful in the storm? Why are you starting this new business at this time when it's not a good time? People telling you to wait. Why are you moving, relocating during this time of uncertainty? How come you're pushing yourself harder now when times are unknown? To an average human, this does not make sense. However, when we have God's favor, it doesn't matter what's going on in the world. It doesn't matter what's going on with the economy; it doesn't matter what's going on with jobs; it doesn't matter what's going on around you. When God gives you favor, nothing matters because at that point you are now backed by the creator who has the power and the ability to do all things at any time. No matter what's going on in the world, we should never forget that he controls the wind, the sun, and all things. He has no restrictions; he has no limitations; he has the power to set you apart in uncertain times; he has the power to walk you through a storm gracefully; he has the power to give you blessings that people will never be able to understand; he has the power to bless you in this season of darkness. Even in this drought, he has the power to give you joy when there's nothing but sadness around you. He has the power to lift you up when everybody is down. He has the power to bless you financially when the world is going through financial hardship. When you have God's favor, there are no limitations. It's very important that we understand the benefits of trusting God in our lives and understanding how he works. Yes, we become emotional and get scared. Yes, we see a lot of things going on around us, but that has nothing to do with God's ability to give you favor if he sees fit. Once you have God's favor, nothing around you can stop it.

I remember having conversations with my wife about the news. Every time we were turning the television on, we would just see one crazy story after another. It seemed like it was all surrounding the world and people were getting ill and dying, losing their jobs, small businesses were crashing. It was just hell looking at television. When I talked to my wife about these things going on in the world, the kids were not going back to school, forced to homeschool. Everything went virtual, everything was shut down. I told my wife, "It's a lot going on in the world."

"Yes," she replied, "we all are a little weary."

However, remember God is in control of all things and we have his favor. God loves us and he's going to take care of his children. Even though there is a lot going on in the news with so much unfairness and people hurting, in these times we have to remember that God works best during uncertain times. In my life, I have learned that God loves to show what he's capable of doing in our lives for other people to see his glory. He wants others to see his blessings. In those moments, we have the ability to bring more people to him because people will clearly see the life that you're living and all of the things that are happening for you. When the world appears to be falling apart, blessings have to come from a higher power. The interesting part is that you never know what, who, how and where your blessings will come from. They will come through during those times of uncertainty in the world.

In a time of uncertainty, God has the power to use even your enemies, even someone who may not have the same beliefs, even someone who you may have had a falling out with, even someone who may not even support you, to bless you. That's why it's very important that we walk in love at all times. What I've learned is that even if you're having a moment to yourself, you're agitated, or you're not in the mood, still walk in love. If you're having a crazy day and just need some help, support, or advice, still walk in love, because you never know who's going to be used to bless you in the uncertain time. There are some people who society looks down on or may judge, but your blessings could come from a criminal, a homeless person, a liar, a thief, a drug addict, an alcoholic, a gang member, a pastor, an elderly person—you never know who God will use to bless you in these moments.

This is why we have to walk in love even when we don't feel like it or feel alone, hurt, frustrated, lost and confused. We must walk in love and walk in forgiveness just like these scriptures mention.

1 Corinthians 16:14 (ESV): "Let all that you do be done in love."

1 John 2:10 (ESV): "Whoever loves his brother abides in the light, and in him there is no cause for stumbling."

1 Corinthians 13:13 (ESV): "So now faith, hope, and love abide, these three; but the greatest of these is love."

1 Corinthians 13:4-7 (NIV): "Love is patient, love is kind. It does not envy, it does not boast, it is not proud. It does not dishonor others, it is not self-seeking, it is not easily angered, it keeps no record of wrongs. Love does not delight in evil but rejoices with the truth. It always protects, always trusts, always hopes, always perseveres."

Psalm 30:5 (NIV): "For his anger last only a moment but his favor lasts a lifetime; weeping may stay for the night, but rejoicing comes in the morning."

Psalm 106:4 (ESV): "Remember me, O Lord, when you show favor to your people; help me when you save them."

Numbers 6:25-26 (ESV): "The Lord make his face to shine upon you and be gracious to you; the Lord lift up his countenance upon you and give you peace."

Psalm 86:17 (NKJV): "Show me a sign for good, that those who hate me may see it and be ashamed, because You, Lord, have helped me and comforted me."

Psalm 84:11 (ESV): "For the Lord God is a sun and shield; the Lord bestows favor and honor. No good thing does he withhold from those who walk uprightly."

After reading the scriptures I hope you clearly understand that your blessings have nothing to do with your bank account, status, race, or level of education. When God gives you favor, your blessings no longer come from the physical world but the spiritual world. We work for a living, we go to college to get top degrees, and then we work nonstop. Some of us have multiple businesses, many investments, or none of these things at all. However, the relationship that you have with God will match up because when he gets ready to bless you, he will do it because it's what he wants to do. Nothing can stop it and you don't have to meet a certain qualification for God to give you favor. His favor is undeserving and there's nothing you can do to deserve it. When God is ready to bless you, no devil in hell or on earth can stop you from what he has stored up for you. Some people may look at you, judge you, and wonder why you are so successful or so happy. Why is it that everybody else is losing and you're winning? Why is it that you walk around with a smile on your face? One thing people forget is we all have an opportunity to have a relationship with our heavenly Father, and that relationship is not always a public relationship. Sometimes, people tend to judge you, not knowing that you could be a person who has a relationship with your Father. I think it's a matter of people looking at you and thinking to themselves that you're not perfect in their eyes. God knows your heart, he knows your story, struggles, pain, challenges, and everything else about you. Other people may not even know he knows everything you've gone through. Your whole life from the outside looking in seems easy for someone to judge you and not understand you, but God sees right through the heart. We all have our problems; we are all sinners and only by his grace are we forgiven. **John 8:7 KJV:** "So when they continued asking him, he lifted up himself, and said unto them, He that is without sin among you, let him first cast a stone at her."

What does "Let he without sin" mean?

"Phrase: Let him who is without sin cast the first stone. Only those who are faultless have the right to pass judgement upon others (implying that no one is faultless and that, therefore, no one had such a right to pass judgement)" (Wiktionary.org).

"Also, you are not too dirty for God to cleanse. You are not too broken for God to fix. You are not too far for God to reach. You are not too guilty for God to forgive. You are not too worthless for God to love." *Christian Rider Cory*

Romans 8:38-39 NLT: "And I am convinced that nothing can ever separate us from God's love. Neither death nor life, neither angels nor demons, neither our fears for today nor our worries about tomorrow—not even the powers of hell can separate us from God's love. No power in the sky above or in the earth below—indeed, nothing in all creation will ever be able to separate us from the love of God that is revealed in Christ Jesus our Lord."

Read Psalm 27:1-14 when the test of time comes your way:

Psalm 27:1-14 KJV:

27 The Lord is my light and my salvation; whom shall I fear? the Lord is the strength of my life; of whom shall I be afraid?

2 When the wicked, even mine enemies and my foes, came upon me to eat up my flesh, they stumbled and fell.

3 Though an host should encamp against me, my heart shall not fear: though war should rise against me, in this will I be confident.

4 One thing have I desired of the Lord, that will I seek after; that I may dwell in the house of the Lord all the

days of my life, to behold the beauty of the Lord, and to enquire in his temple.

5 For in the time of trouble he shall hide me in his pavilion: in the secret of his tabernacle shall he hide me; he shall set me up upon a rock.

6 And now shall mine head be lifted up above mine enemies round about me: therefore will I offer in his tabernacle sacrifices of joy; I will sing, yea, I will sing praises unto the Lord.

7 Hear, O Lord, when I cry with my voice: have mercy also upon me, and answer me.

8 When thou saidst, seek ye my face; my heart said unto thee, Thy face, Lord, will I seek.

9 Hide not thy face far from me; put not thy servant away in anger: thou hast been my help; leave me not, neither forsake me, O God of my salvation.

10 When my father and my mother forsake me, then the Lord will take me up.

11 Teach me thy way, O Lord, and lead me in a plain path, because of mine enemies.

12 Deliver me not over unto the will of mine enemies: for false witnesses are risen up against me, and such as breathe out cruelty.

13 I had fainted, unless I had believed to see the goodness of the Lord in the land of the living.

14 Wait on the Lord: be of good courage, and he shall strengthen thine heart: wait, I say, on the Lord.

CHAPTER 20

Take the Attention off Yourself: Your Season of Challenges Is Other People's Everyday Life

Your blessing could be standing right in front of you, just turn around and look away from yourself and turn towards someone who may need you more than you may know it. Even in your craziest times, you can still be a blessing to someone else, and that person could be holding the key to unlocking your favor with God. Sometimes, in uncertainty we are tested to see if we really understand what God's word is all about.

Deuteronomy 15:11 NIV: "There will always be poor people in the land. Therefore I command you to be open-handed toward your fellow Israelites who are poor and needy in your land."

Isaiah 58:10 ESV: "If you pour yourself out for the hungry and satisfy the desire of the afflicted, then shall your light rise in the darkness and your gloom be as the noonday."

Proverbs 19:17 NIV: "Whoever is kind to the poor lends to the Lord, and he will reward them for what they have done."

Luke 6:38 NIV: "Give, and it will be given to you. A good measure, pressed down, shaken together and running over, will be poured into your lap. For with the measure you use, it will be measured to you."

I wanted to write this part of the book to give you a different perspective on the challenges you may be facing. During my many obstacles, I actually experienced a lot of joy by simply taking the attention off of myself and turning it towards others. I have to be real; I was in a really broken place at that time. However, I knew that someone else really needed me and I had nothing to lose being a blessing to them. We have to be prepared to give someone else words of encouragement even when we've lost our own selves. One day I needed help. I didn't have much money—I may have only had about $20 to my name—and something in my heart moved me to help someone who was outside of a store. I ended up paying for their food. Honestly, I didn't have enough money left over for myself.

However, God opened the floodgates and started maneuvering things in my life. The crazy part is, the person who I bought food for had no idea I was actually going through it myself. But because I put others before myself, I took the attention off myself. God started blessing me in ways I couldn't imagine. Never forget there could be someone right now in the same situation that may need a message from you. Maybe they need prayer or maybe they need to hear your stories of faith to overcome their obstacles.

CHAPTER 21
20/20 Vision

What does it mean to have 20/20 vision? 20/20 vision is a term used to express normal visual acuity (the clarity or sharpness of vision) measured at a distance of 20 feet. If you have 20/20 vision, you can see clearly at 20 feet, with both eyes, what should normally be seen at that distance (American Optometric Association – www.aoa.org).

Now let's look at this from a different standpoint. According to the *Evangelical Dictionary of Biblical Theology*, visions often occur in the Bible as instruments of supernatural revelation. In both the old and new testaments, vision is the act of seeing, observing, or perceiving. In the Old Testament, visions were often used to receive a divine word. I remember going into the year 2020, everyone was saying, "2020 perfect vision, this is going to be a great year; this is going to be the year that we see the truth in everything." Unfortunately, the vision that many of us had for ourselves would suddenly stop! Putting the entire world in a position that only God could save us. I guess what I'm trying to say is man could have a vision for himself, plans for himself, have hopes and dreams for himself, but God also has them for us. In order for you to hear God's voice to receive God's visions, you have to spend time with God. That's what this worldwide pandemic did for us; the world was shut down and we were all forced to stay in the house and talk to God. It gave many people an opportunity to seek him and get to know him. None of us had any answers at this moment, we needed all the help and answers. We needed to hear God's voice in a way that we'd never heard it before! So many nights, I would just pray and ask God to just show me something, and I'd turn to the Bible where it was clear. Dreams come to us during sleep, but visions occur when we are awake. As **Numbers 24:4 KJV** states: "He hath said, which heard the words of God, which saw the vision of the Almighty, falling into a trance, but having his eyes open." God uses dreams to speak to us and reveal his plans. Our spirit has direct communications with him to make us aware of possible trouble coming our way. Prophetic revelations give us battle strategies. Visions have a different purpose. God uses visions to reveal himself and his glory, to make himself known. When I think back over my life, I had so many visions. I had so many thoughts racing through my mind. I felt deep down inside that the gift that I had was not to be used for me, but to be used to bring glory to God. However, I kept pushing it off and running around the mulberry bush. When the pandemic hit, it forced me to be quiet and stop talking. I focused on hearing God's voice, and saw that it's almost impossible to have God's vision if you're too busy for him. In order to have God's vision, you must get to know him and understand how he works. Then, you shall hear his voice from the heavens.

Epilogue

I thank you so much for reading my book. This is my third published book, and I must say it means the most to me. I hope and pray that after reading this book, you make a decision to get closer to God and build a personal relationship with him. Trust me when I tell you, there's nothing like it. I spent many years having lots of anxiety and it was like I was in uncertain times every day. I had to make a decision to walk with God. That's when things slowly got better for me. I ask you today to make a decision to let him into your life and try him. Have faith that, in times of uncertainty, and in the darkest moments of confusion, pain, sorrow, hurt and disappointment, he will not leave you or forsake you. Remember as it says in the word, God is always present. Even in a pandemic. Even when you're all alone, all you have to do is call on him and he will answer you. Take one step, and he will take the next step with you. Be blessed and thank you for reading my book.

JOURNAL

Challenging times will show up in life, anticipate them, and prepare yourself.

List 10 things you have learned from reading this book that you believe will help you overcome the unknown, no matter what challenges come your way.

_____

_____

_____

_____

_____

_____

What are some of the challenges you are currently facing?

After you list them, go back to the book and go through the chapters, list scriptures that you have learned, then write them down and repeat them every single day until you memorize them and you're able to use them as a weapon to protect yourself during times of difficulty.

_____

_____

_____

_____

_____

_____

_____

_____

_____

_____

_____

_____

_____

_____

_____

_____

_____

_____

_____

_____

_____

There is a lesson in everything, even your darkest moments. Take the next few pages and write lessons that you've learned in your experience. Then write something about this moment that opened your eyes to see things that you may not have seen before that you feel will bless you moving forward.

_____

_____

_____

_____

_____

_____

_____

_____

_____

_____

_____

_____

_____

_____

_____

_____

_____

_____

_____

_____

_____

_____

_____

_____

_____

_____

_____

_____

_____

_____

_____

_____

_____

_____

_____

The sun always shines after the storm, even if it's not on your terms. God is always present.

Write as many reasons as you can of why it's worth staying strong and never giving up in the middle of a storm, based on what you've read in this book.

_____

_____

_____

_____

_____

_____

_____

_____

_____

Blessings in Uncertain Times

_____

_____

_____

_____

_____

_____

_____

_____

_____

_____

_____

_____

_____

_____

2020 Experience

Write down your 2020 God experience and use it as a testimony to uplift others in their time of need.

Write and keep this for the rest of your life so you will never forget the blessings and the favor of God in uncertain times. After you write your experience, congratulations, you will have written your first book that will be your blueprint and roadmap for whenever storms come your way. You will have the book to reflect upon when life doesn't make sense. You will be able to go back and read your 2020 God experience and it will be a reminder that God is always in control no matter what.

_____

_____

_____

_____

_____

_____

_____

_____

_____

_____

_____

_____

_____

_____

_____

_____

_____

_____

_____

_____

_____

_____

_____

_____

_____

_____

_____

_____

_____

_____

_____

_____

_____

_____

_____

_____

_____

_____

_____

_____

_____

_____

_____

_____

_____

_____

_____

_____

_____

_____

_____

_____

_____

_____

_____

_____

CPSIA information can be obtained
at www.ICGtesting.com
Printed in the USA
LVHW101120210421
684110LV00009B/6/J